# VAUDEVILLE FOR A PRINCESS

# Books by *Delmore Schwartz*

*In Dreams Begin Responsibilities*

*Shenandoah*

*Genesis*

*The World Is A Wedding*

IN PREPARATION   *T. S. Eliot*

*Selected Writings*

*Delmore Schwartz*

# VAUDEVILLE FOR A PRINCESS
## AND OTHER POEMS

A New Directions Book

ACKNOWLEDGMENT

Some of the material in this volume was first published in the magazines: *Partisan Review, Horizon, Kenyon Review, Commentary, Poetry: A Magazine of Verse,* and *Accent.*

MANUFACTURED IN THE UNITED STATES
*New Directions Books are published by James Laughlin*
NEW YORK OFFICE — 333 SIXTH AVENUE

—I think that now we who are together this evening cannot find anything better to do than to praise Love.

I propose that each of us, speaking in turn, going from left to right, make a speech in praise and celebration of Love.

—Who can have any objection? said Socrates. Certainly I cannot since I profess to understand nothing but matters of Love.

For if I have not been talking about Love all the time, what have I been talking about, anyway?

# Contents

# VAUDEVILLE FOR A PRINCESS

SUGGESTED BY PRINCESS
ELIZABETH'S ADMIRATION
OF DANNY KAYE

Vive la bagatelle — *Swift*

Imagine for my purpose that you are
a squad of urchins — *Joyce*

"True eloquence mocks eloquence."
    Did that Frenchman mean
That heroes are hilarious
    And orators obscene?

Eloquence laughs at rhetoric,
    Is ill at ease in Zion,
Or baa-baas like the lucid lamb,
    And snickers at the lion,

And smiles, being meticulous,
Because truth is ridiculous.

Is it not true that the discussion of the meaning of existentialism has been dying down? or at any rate is being taken more and more for granted, like cynicism, optimism, surrealism, alcoholism, and practically all other well-known topics of conversation?

If so, this is a dangerous state of affairs. For as soon as a philosophy is taken for granted, as soon as its meaning is assumed, then it begins to be misunderstood and misinterpreted. Philosophical idealism is a good example. It was once just as fashionable as existentialism and is now generally thought to have to do with those impractical people who believe in ideals and never amount to anything.

I propose a revival of interest in the meaning of existentialism because when everyone asks what something means, the possibilities of misunderstanding are, if not lessened, more controllable. Having studied existentialism in an offhand way since 1935, I become more and more convinced that its meaning can be reduced to the following formulation: *Existentialism means that no one else can take a bath for you.*

This example is suggested by Heidegger, who points out that no one else can die for you. You must die your own death. But the same is true of taking a bath. And I prefer the bath as an example to death because, as Heidegger further observes, no one likes to think very much about death, except indigent undertakers perhaps. Death is for most a distant event, however unpleasant and inevitable.

A bath, however, is a daily affair, at least in America. Thus it is something you have to think about somewhat everyday, and while you are thinking about it, and while, perforce, you are taking a bath, you might just as well be thinking about what existentialism means. Otherwise you will probably just be thinking about yourself, which is narcissism; or about other human beings, which is likely to be malicious, unless you are feeling very good; or worst of all, you may not be thinking at all, which is senseless and a waste of time.

Of course, there are other acts which each human being must perform for himself, such as eating, breathing, sleeping, making love, etc. But taking a bath seems to me the best of the lot because it involves the vital existentialist emphasis on choice: you can choose *not* to take a bath, you can waver in your choice, you can finally decide to take a bath, the whole drama of human freedom can become quite hectic or for that matter quite boring. But eating is hardly a matter of choice, except for the menu itself, nor is breathing which can be done not only without taking thought but while one is quite unconscious. As for making love, taking a bath is a better example because you can keep it clean, simple, free of fixations, perversions, inhibitions and an overpowering sense of guilt.

Now despite the fact that most of the bathtubs which exist are in America, some Americans are not in the habit of taking baths for granted. I know of one American (formerly an existentialist, by the way) who avoids taking frequent baths because he feels that the taking of a bath is an *extreme situation.* (He is not averse to using existentialist arguments when it suits his torso, though in company he attacks existentialism). He says that taking a bath is an extreme situation because God knows what may occur to you when you are in the tub, you may decide to drown yourself because existence, as existentialists say, is essentially *absurd;* you may decide to become a narcissist because of the pleasures of the warm and loving water. But there's no use listing all the catastrophes this fellow thinks may occur to anyone in the extreme situation of taking a bath.

So too with the bathtaking of a close friend of mine, who finds the taking of baths a matter of no little thought. He takes two baths a day, but he has to force himself to do so because there are so many other more important things to do (so it seems to him!) or which he feels he ought to do during the time occupied in taking a bath (note how the question of moral value enters at this point). It is a matter for much thought also because he has to decide whether to take a bath or a shower. He is afraid that sooner or later he will break his neck slipping on a cake of soap while taking a shower (which he prefers to a bath), although, on the other hand, he feels that in some ways it is better to take a shower than a bath because then he does not have to wash out the tub for others (*the others* are always important, as Sartre has observed), and in short the taking of baths is not a simple matter for him. Once I visited him while he was taking a shower, and while I was conversing with his wife in their handsome living-room, he kept crying out through the downpour of the shower: "Say, you know it's mighty lonesome in here." He wanted me to visit with him and keep him company (note the *aloneness* of the human situation as depicted by the existentialists), to converse with him. Consequently, after he had shouted his fourth appeal for my company, I had to go in and point out to him that we would have to shout at each other because of the noise of the shower and we shouted at each other often enough for more justifiable reasons.

In the upper class, as is well known, it is customary (I am told by friends who have soared to these circles at times ho, ho!) to take at least two baths a day, while in the lower middle class and working class this is less true, an observation I bring forward to show how important social and economic factors are, or, as the existentialists say, how all being is being-in-the-world, although they seem to think that the social and economic aspects of being-in-the-world are not so important as I am forced to think they are. Of course, some of the existentialists may have changed their minds during the second World War and the recent so-called peace.

The real difficulty in explaining what existentialism means flows from the basis of this philosophy, a basis which can be summarized in the following proposition: *Human beings exist.* They have an existence which is human and thus different from that of stones, trees, animals, cigar store Indians, and numerous human beings who are trying their best not to exist or not to be human.

If you are really human, if you really exist as a human being, you have no need of any explanation of existence or existentialism. In the meantime, the best thing to do is to keep on reading explanations of existentialism and existence.

As for me, I never take baths. Just showers. Takes less time.

The mind to me a North Pole is,
Superb the whiteness there I find,
The glaring snows of consciousness
Dazzle enough to make me blind,
Until I see too much, in this
Resembling James' governess.

❀      ❀      ❀

The mind and self in Civil War
Are locked and wasted, blocked and forced.
Desire raids the heart once more,
As scruple counts desire's cost.
Each day betrays the night's last dream,
While night confuses same and seem.

Now Jackson raids the Shenandoah,
Now ironclads block the Southern coast,
Sharp England keeps shop, seeking power.
At Gettysburg both sides are lost.
From London, Marx computes the cost,
Young Adams finds it all a bore.

Perfidious Albion hesitates.
Brady takes death's true photographs.
Charles Adams' tact transforms the fates.
Lincoln tells jokes but no one laughs.
Grant gets drunk as the rocking sea:
Ulysses longs for his family.

Who pardons the weak who fall asleep?
Lincoln forgives the Gorgon's commands,
Procrastinates, and fears to leap,

Knowing how little he understands.
Triumph appears ambiguous:
How nervous are his shaky hands.

Davis protects his friends to the end.
The Negroes chant in the promised land,
The Negroes jig at heaven's gates,
Lincoln explains why he hesitates,
What right which wrong attack defends,
And who with what will make amends.

This is the famous Civil War.
Assassins stop in Baltimore.
Grant closes in remorsefully,
Longing for home and family,
As Lincoln sighs for unity
Until Booth kills him pointlessly.

      ❖    ❖    ❖

The mind resembles all creation,
The mind is all things, in a way:
Deceptive as pure observation,
Heartbreaking as a tragic play.
Idle, denial; false, affirmation;
And vain the heart's imagination—
    Unless or if on Judgment Day
    When God says what He has to say.

Cars are very important, even if one does not care very much about cars. This is because most people admire a handsome car very much. If one is an owner of a fine car, then one is regarded by the populace in general as being very successful and prosperous.

I myself never cared very much for cars, but as the years pass I can see how serious and significant a part they have played in my life. In 1929 when my family was rich, or supposed to be rich, I was given the gift of a Chrysler royal coupe, brand-new. I did not know how to drive and our chauffeur had to teach me and the first thing I did at the wheel, turning the corner, was to drive into a truck, but slowly, so nothing bad happened. I have hardly had any accidents since then, for this beginning made me very cautious. I wanted to give up driving right then and there, but the wise chauffeur insisted that I continue, or otherwise I would never be able to drive a car.

I was full of pride in this beautiful car and went about in it, trying to find girls to ride with me and a friend. We were not very successful because we drove down Riverside Drive and the girls loitering there invariably preferred sailors when the fleet was in town. My friend said that this was because the navy spent money freely and without a care. Be this as it may, the car caused me no little sorrow because I expected girls to be very much attracted by it, but instead they were suspicious, cautious, and thought my friend and I eager only to make love. This was true enough, but what about the sailors?

After two years during which time I suffered at the hands of the fair sex and also suffered because I expected girls to fall for my car, and suffered also because I was driving without a license and scared by every cop who glanced at me, I had to sell my car to pay my tuition fees at the university where I was supposed to be studying. I was cheated in the deal, but that's another story. The main point is that the depression had begun and that my family was not rich, as had been supposed, and I did not have the money to pay for the upkeep of the car.

It took me five years to get used to the idea that I was not what a relative termed a rich heir and the idea that the depression was not just an interval before a new period of prosperity. By that time I had accustomed myself to the idea of being without a car. All I wanted to do was to read books.

By 1938, I had read so many books that I wrote one. I felt so good that I went out and bought a car, a 1929 Ford. It was a good car, despite it's age, and it gave me much pleasure and fostered no foolish, amorous expectations. At the end of the year I sold it for twenty-five dollars in credit. I was cheated again by an automobile dealer wise in the ways of the world. But still the car was a good thing.

In 1939, I lived during the winter at a summer resort and had to buy a car again and I bought a 1928 Chevrolet. This was the best of all the cars so far as satisfaction went, although the motor was not all that it should have been. Driving from place to place in this car, I secured a very fine job, a much desired prize, and visited many illustrious and interesting persons. One of them was much struck by the fact that I drove a car at all. After I had visited him at his summer house in the mountains, he said to a friend of mine: *"He can drive a car!"* This shows the kind of impression I make on most human beings, partly because I look shy and helpless. I look that way very often because I am trying to figure out why the Giants did not win the pennant in 1928, or what would have happened if Germany had won the First World War, or what would have happened to me if not for the great depression which stopped me from being a rich young man. I also think of other things like that and find myself fascinated by all kinds of possibilities, if indeed they are possibilities. Strange that my abstracted and absent-minded look should make people think that I am shy and helpless: do they think I am not thinking *at all?* The fact is, I am passionate with reveries of glory and power, of riding up Fifth Avenue under great snowstorms of ticker-tape, in a beautiful open limousine, cheered by admiring throngs.

Anyway, I had to sell my third car, the 1928 Chevrolet, in 1940, because the police in the city in which I lived kept giving me tickets for parking outdoors all night, but I had to, for I did not have the money to pay for a garage. After the sale was concluded — and this time I was very cautious and cagey with the used car dealer — I felt that I was really slipping. After eleven years I had no car and I did not see how I was going to have a car very soon, but I had begun in 1929 with a very fine 1929 car.

Taxis are better, and less expensive, I figured during this period.

During the war a very rich friend often lent me his very expensive car, for at this time I was trying to impress a very cold and handsome young lady. She was not impressed since she did not like the way that I drove, and the truth is that my skill had decayed because of insufficient practice and because I had become very nervous as a result of all the ups and downs of life as I had known it.

Things went from worse to worst. I became so nervous that I was afraid to drive a car. But then at the darkest hour, I decided to buy a new car. This was quite recently, and the car belonged to a prosperous friend of mine who was afraid to sell it to me being aware of how nervous I was and thinking as others have that I was not the sort who could drive a car very well. He asked me politely if I still remembered how to drive, for he had seen me driving and had sat next to me in my 1928 Chevrolet in 1939. The sale was consummated after his natural hesitancy and the customary formalities. I secured an ownership license, license plates, and I would have taken a road test for a driver's license — my first one had expired four years before — except that one had to wait two weeks for an appointment and I had to go out of town immediately.

So there I was on the road again. Allons! I said to myself, as Walter Whitman used to say, once more without a driver's license just like in 1929 when I was too young to be permitted to get one in the state of New York which is very strict. And my emotions were pretty much the same, — *le plus ça change, le plus c'est la même chose* — fear of the cops, bravado based on the probability and improbability of being halted, nervousness which doubtless went back to the strain of being hauled with great difficulty into this brave new world (it was a spectacular labor, I am told, and it was not until my mother accidentally kicked her father's photograph off the bedroom wall that the doctor said to my dubious and anxious father that everyone was going to be all right, a

**11**

superficial remark if I ever heard one). Nevertheless, I drove with ever-increasing composure, and even, one might go so far as to say, a certain serenity, poise and power, going north, and feeling very good, despite the illegal character of my activity. For it had occurred to me to think of my first three cars, and when I compared them with this new car, I was very pleased. First the 1929 royal coupe in 1929, next the 1929 Ford in 1930, third the 1928 Chevrolet in 1939-40, but now, after so many years of poverty and various kinds of oppression, chiefly internal, I owned a 1936 Buick in 1949.

There is no reason for wild optimism, but it would be hard to deny that I am slowly inching my way forward. It is true that this car is thirteen years old and at worst in the past my car was no more than twelve years old. But a Buick is a far, far better car than a Chevrolet, and next year if all goes well I think I may very well be able to trade it in for a 1941 Studebaker, with a radio and clock that really work. If this fair hope is fulfilled, I will only be nine years behind my starting point in 1929 and this will be progress indeed and who knows what the future may hold, so far as used cars go?

When that I was and a little tiny boy,
　With a hey ho, the wind and the rain,
I did not know the truth of joy,
　I thought that life was passed in pain.

And when I came to thought and art,
　Shame made my naive flowers wilt,
I glowed disgusted with my heart,
　As cynicism salved my guilt.

When youthful hopes proved true and false,
　As hard-earned riches fool or pall,
I thought the mind lied like a waltz
　Which chants love as a brilliant ball.

And when I followed where sleep fled
　I woke amid the mixing dream,
My self or others hurt my head,
　Making the frigid Furies scream.

And when I fled from this estate,
　I drove the quickest car to bliss,
With drunken fools I struck at fate,
　Charmed at the falls of consciousness.

A great while ago the world began,
　With a ho ho, the fog and the mist,
The Pharaohs are enthroned again,
　The endless wind and rain persist.

Illusion and madness dim the years
   Mere parodies of hope, at best,
And yet through all these mounting fears
   How I am glad that I exist!

How strange the truth appears at last!
   I feel as old as outworn shoes,
I know what I have lost or missed
   Or certainly will some day lose

And yet this knowledge, like the Jews,
   Can make me glad that I exist!
      with a hey ho, the stupid past,
        and a ho ho, and a ha ha at last.

Hamlet came from an old upper-class family. He was the only son of a king. He was very intelligent, though somewhat of an intellectual, and he was quite handsome too, except for a tendency to get fat in the face and thicken. The Prime Minister Polonius itched with an eagerness to get Hamlet to marry his beautiful, charming and sweet-tempered daughter Ophelia. Not only that, but more important by far, Ophelia was very much in love with Hamlet, and when Hamlet went to Germany to study metaphysics and lager beer, she thought about him all the time. "That's what love or infatuation seems to me," said Ophelia, "it's when you think of someone all the time, wondering what the loved one is thinking, what he is doing, and if he will ever love you the way you love him," which is not very likely, most things tending to be one-sided affairs.

Hamlet's father, the king, died suddenly, and right after the funeral, Hamlet's mother remarried, her new husband being Claudius, the king's brother who now became king himself. The marriage took place very soon after the funeral and Hamlet was enraged and it was then that Hamlet began to behave in a most peculiar manner much to everyone's surprise and perplexity. He had always been very careful about his appearance, even somewhat of a dandy: now he looked like someone who has slept for three nights in a railroad coach, and slept very poorly at that. He had always been consistently sensible, polite and full of tact. Now he made all kinds of remarks which no one could understand, and he went about looking very glum, but it was better when he was glum because when he opened his mouth, he said something which seemed, at best, mysterious, and often enough, maniacal. For example, when his mother said that he ought not to be so sad about his father's death, because the show must go on, life is full of inevitable losses, everyone is bound to die, sooner or later, what did Hamlet say in answer? He requested his mother to sing for him as she had when he was a child, the old songs "My Old Kentucky Womb," and "Carry Me Back To Old Virginity." Naturally she did not know what to make of this.

Some people thought that he was behaving like that because he was very much in love with Ophelia. But that's ridiculous. Ophelia would have married him without hesitation. And even those who thought that he was just a lovesick young man were not sure of this explanation and went about eavesdropping and looking through transoms each time Hamlet and Ophelia were alone with each other.

Other people, particularly Claudius his uncle the new king thought that Hamlet was very angry because he wanted to be king himself. Claudius thought that everyone was just like he was, for he had wanted to be king very much.

The truth is that Hamlet did not care about being king because he was very depressed about everything. He just felt rotten, no matter what he did. And when he talked to his best friend Horatio, or visited with his old friend the local undertaker, what he talked about in the main was how depressed he was, how meaningless life seemed to him, and how he would like to commit suicide.

"There's an eternity that mocks our hopes," he said one day to Horatio, "no matter what we try." This was supposed to explain why he did not commit suicide, even though he felt like it. Horatio was polite, so he did not tell Hamlet that he did not understand a word of what he was saying.

Some people supposed that his mother's second marriage, and right after the funeral of his father, was what upset Hamlet so much. It is certainly true that Hamlet did behave in an extraordinary and offensive way with his mother, telling her that she had married too soon, that her new husband and his uncle was far from being as fine a man as his father had been, and that she ought not to let her new husband make love to her, among other ridiculous suggestions. According to this view of his conduct, he was jealous of his uncle and in love with his mother, who was still a very attractive woman.

There may be a great deal of truth in this view of Hamlet's behavior, for all we know, but then again how about his father? He never behaved like that when his father was alive, nor did he carry on in a sullen and disgruntled manner, not even as an infant. Still and all, this may be a superficial difficulty in observing Hamlet's true state of mind, for he was certainly horrified by the very idea of his uncle just touching his mother.

He said to her in fury one night in her bedroom, — *to live,*

> *In the rank sweat of an enseaméd bed,*
> *Stewed in corruption, honeying, and making love*
> *Over the nasty sty.*

And many more remarks of the same kind, just as adolescent and irritating, indicating that he had a distinct aversion, to say the least, to the idea of people making love. Love seems to have been something dirty to him, in fact, a four letter word: L-O-V-E.

But something more than this incestuous jealousy was wrong with Hamlet, as you can see when you know that he told the sweet and likable Ophelia to become a nun. It's one thing to turn a girl down, but to make these proposals about her future, a future with which you refused to have anything to do, is quite insulting and shows how disgusted Hamlet was with the idea of anyone making love to anyone else. Probably he wanted Ophelia to become a nun so that no one would ever make love to her. And Horatio, who was a kind and well-meaning fellow, as well as a good friend, said to Hamlet that he had been very cruel to Ophelia and that he ought not to mistreat a girl just because she was very much in love with him.

"A pretty girl is like a canteloupe," replied Hamlet, "once opened, begins to get rotten." What kind of a remark was that for a well-bred young man to make?

Horatio just sighed when he heard such things, for he realized that his friend was under a severe emotional strain.

"You never step twice into the same girl, as Heraclitus should have said," Hamlet continued, now that he was on the subject of girls. "I would like something more permanent."

"You did not always feel like this," Horatio remarked, "perhaps this is just a passing phase?"

Hamlet shrugged his shoulders and expressed contempt for his uncle the king on the ground that he drank too much.

"Those whom the gods would destroy, they first make successful," said Hamlet, apropos of nothing at all and at the same time everything, including his uncle's success and alcoholism for he had become more

**17**

and more given to statements of a quasi-philosophical and invariably cynical character.

"You better watch those human relationships," said Horatio, thinking again of how cruel Hamlet had been to Ophelia.

"That's what upset me so much," Hamlet fatuously replied, "I've been watching those human relationships, and I do not like them very much."

You can see how sick a young man he was also when you remember how beautiful, lovable, and delightful a creature Ophelia was. She would have done anything to make Hamlet happy. The fact that she was in love with him made absolutely no impact on him, except perhaps to irritate him because it was a distraction from what really preoccupied him.

"I had not thought life has undone so many," said Hamlet to Horatio and to Ophelia, in passing.

Some people also thought that Hamlet suspected his uncle of killing his father in order to get his throne and his wife, and consequently the reason that he felt badly and behaved strangely was that he felt that he ought to avenge his father's murder but suffered from a lack of will-power. But he did not suffer from lack of will-power, nor was he a coward, as some have supposed. This should be obvious because when he was sent to England by his uncle, ostensibly for a change of scene to improve his health and emotions, and when he found out that this trip was really a plot to get him killed in England, he acted swiftly, bravely, and with resolution, stealing the secret papers which contained orders to have him killed and fixing it so that his accompanists, who were in the pay of his uncle, would be wiped out instead of him: *hardly* the behavior of a coward with no will-power!

It's true that he was disturbed by his father's death and detested his uncle but this hardly explains his state of mind, and he killed a man suddenly because he was eavesdropping behind the curtain when he was talking to his mother. He thought the spy was his uncle, but it was Ophelia's father, poor Polonius. Ophelia went insane quite reasonably because the man she loved had killed her father and she was in an inexorable emotional trap, from which she fled by means of drowning herself, an event which brought her brother back from his studies in France to challenge Hamlet to a duel. But as a result of tricky and despicable Claudius' machinations, this duel resulted in a virtual holocaust: everyone was stabbed or poisoned to death, except Horatio.

People have been arguing for hundreds of years about what was really wrong with Hamlet. Some say that he must have been a woman, some say that he was homosexual, in love with his uncle or with Horatio, and unable to bear the fact that his uncle slept with a woman, and there is one fascinating view which maintains that all the mystery is utterly clarified if we suppose that everyone is roaring drunk from the beginning to the end of the play. This view is very fine except that I don't see how it clarifies anything, for drunk or sober, not everyone behaves the same, and the real question is why Hamlet behaved as he did: certainly just hitting the bottle does not account for all his emotions and opinions, and *in vino veritas,* anyway.

Needless to say, I have a theory too; in fact, several. But I don't know if it is correct or not? For if after all these years no one has explained why Hamlet felt as he did, it does not seem very likely that I can. However, for what it is worth, and to use clinical terms, I will say in brief that I think Hamlet suffered from a well-known pathological disorder. He was manic; and he was depressive. No one knows what the real causes of the manic-depressive disorder are, whether physical or mental or both, and that is why no one understands Hamlet.

Now that is my point, the fact that you can have this gift or that disease, and no one understands why, no one is responsible, and no one can really alter matters, and yet no one can stop thinking that someone is to blame. To be manic-depressive is just like being small or tall, strong, blond, fat, — there is no clear reason for it, it is quite arbitrary, no one seems to have had any choice in the matter, and it is very important, certainly it is very important. This is the reason that the story of Hamlet is very sad, bad and immoral. It has all these traits because Hamlet's diseased emotions caused the deaths of the beautiful Ophelia, her pompous but well-meaning father, her hot-headed brother Laertes, and his own talented self. In this way we must recognize the fact that there is something wrong with everyone and everything.

We poets by the past and future used
Stare east and west distractedly at times,
Knowing there are, in fullness and in flower,
Chrysanthemums and Mozart in the room,
A stillness and a motion, both in bloom.

Or know a girl upon the sofa's ease,
Curved like a stocking, being profoundly round,
As rich and dark as April's underground.
We see in strict perception probity,
The lasting soil and good of all our art,
Which purifies the nervous turned-in heart.

And when we hear in music's empty halls
Torn banners blowing in the rain and shame,
We know these passages are surfaces,
Knowing that our vocation cannot be
Merely a Sunday with the beautiful.
There is pace and grace we must fulfill.

For we must earn through dull dim suffering,
Through ignorance and darkened hope, and hope
Risen again, and clouded over again, and dead despair,
And many little deaths, hardly observed,
The early morning light we have deserved.

It was very nice of the Princess Elizabeth to say something about the problem of marriage and divorce in the modern world. Obviously she had no direct personal stake or bias, because *she* is not going to get a divorce, not after what happened to her Uncle Ed when he wanted to marry a divorced woman: the British Empire will not survive another constitutional crisis like that, no matter how powerful the R. A. F., for though war is worse than divorce, the latter tends to undermine morale. And if we might tend to suppose that Elizabeth did not at the age of 22 have enough experience either in her own life or through observation of her friends' alliances to discuss these things, nevertheless you can be a good tennis coach, even if you are not a tennis star, so I guess even if you have only been married once and intend to continue, you probably have some sensible points to contribute to the discussion. Anyway, if you are going to be Queen of England, you just have to have decided opinions about practically everything, even if it's only the press agent's prejudices.

Yet I wonder what the future Queen would have to say about the experience of a friend of mine in trying to get a divorce? This friend of mine and his wife had decided to get a divorce because they liked each other very much, but not enough. My friend's wife liked my friend very much, but was unable to get over the fact that he did not resemble Gary Cooper in the least. For one thing, he talked too much while Cooper as is well known is very reticent and at times seems to be tongue-tied. (This lady also liked Conrad Veidt the German film star until the day of his death, and this poses a problem because Veidt also talked a great deal, like her husband, but he spoke with a charming continental accent which made all the difference in the world.)

Well, anyway, when this friend of mine and his wife had decided to get a divorce, they discovered that in the state of New York it was very difficult to get one unless the husband committed bona-fide adultery. If it was not bona-fide, then the judge might get sore, throw the case out of court, and make it impossible for either of the two ever to get a divorce at all, at least in New York. Now my friend was not very much against committing adultery, but he did not like the idea of committing it in cold blood. It reminded him of eating when not hungry. However, his wife's lawyer advised her that this was necessary, and he was insistent. He urged that certain precautions be taken. It was dangerous, he told her, telling her to tell her husband, for her husband to pick up a blonde in a bar, because she might later blackmail him and say that he had not committed bona-fide adultery with her. My friend, hearing this, was very much distressed, because he felt that he just could not ask any other lady he knew to make believe that she was committing adultery with him. It was one thing to get some lady friend to commit adultery. That might take some persuasion but at least it was not insincere and insulting. However, it was something else again to get some friend merely to put in an appearance in a hotel bedroom. She might be very much insulted and offended by the suggestion, which would not make her out to be very attractive, when you consider its implications, I mean the implications of such a proposal. On the other hand, if one did commit adultery, it would be extremely awkward to say the least, to plan to have one's wife come barging in with two witnesses, who, as the lawyer insisted, had to be friends of both. My friend felt that if he went through with a disingenuous performance such as seemed to be necessary, then word might get about that he was merely using his female friends in order to solve and circumvent certain legal difficulties. Besides, he was shy, and he did not want anyone knocking on the hotel door and entering while he and a lady were in a state of disarray, undress and distress.

He discussed the problem with his former-wife-to-be at dinner and she agreed that it was very difficult for him and that he must try to avoid any of the implications of disrespect to his lady friends by proposing that they join with him in this unflattering farce.

After dinner, they joined a married couple who had already consented to be witnesses of my friend's false adultery, and the married couple agreed that there were obvious dangers involved and they sat about in a bar and tried to solve their problem, but they did not seem to be getting anywhere until my friend had what seemed to him a wonderful idea: his wife would commit adultery with him! She would be her own corespondent. They would go, all four, to his hotel suite and she would go to the bedroom, take off her dress, move from the bedroom to the bathroom when the married couple knocked on the door, and being seen in her slip by them as she passed from the bedroom to the bathroom, she might be identified in court as being a woman in a state of undress in my friend's bedroom. What judge in a thousand years would ask the married couple who were going to testify against my friend if they were sure that the woman in undress was not my friend's wife. It just would not occur to any judge? My friend was also delighted by the idea because, just as it seemed to involve no falsification of the truth, so too, in his wife's being her own corespondent, there was a theological parallel he liked very much. It was just like the Father, the Son, and the Holy Ghost!

His wife and the married couple were not as enchanted by this project as he was, but after further discussion, there did not seem anything else to do (except to pick up a blonde and risk blackmail), so they decided to go through with the whole thing, and they did, and they were very nervous and they made nervous jokes such as "who was that corespondent I saw you with in the bedroom?" "That was no corespondent, that was my former wife," but everything turned out very well and at the trial the judge did not ask the testifying witness any simple and direct questions and the divorce was granted, but the wife and the married couple grew very nervous anyway because they thought the scheme was too clever and after the trial they went out to a bar to get a few quick ones because they all had a guilty conscience.

What would the Princess Elizabeth have to say about this ordeal? Would she not have to agree that a divorce, of course, ought not to be made so difficult and should not make necessary so much falsehood or bona-fide adultery? As the divorce laws now stand in the state of New York and in England, I believe, there is implicit in them an open invitation to immorality, if anyone who is sensitive wants to avoid insincerity, perjury, disingenuity, and insults to members of the opposite sex. Of course, her main point was that people ought not to get divorced at all, but since this would only lead to more and more adultery, judging by the facts, she would be caught on the horns of a dilemma.

However, it must be admitted that of late divorce too has become very peculiar. People not only take marriage lightly, they also seem to be incapable of taking a divorce very seriously. For example, two, not only one, of my acquaintances, have shown a tendency to visit their former wives after the divorce has gone through and to spend the night with them. One of them explained to me that after you have been married for a long time, you form certain habits which tend to continue in spite of the fact that you have been divorced, which tends to seem somewhat of a legal abstraction, especially since you get along so well with your former wife when the chief obstacle to getting along with her, marriage, has been removed. The other acquaintance who was a victim of this habit was very shamefaced about it, however. He claimed that he had stayed overnight because he could not get a room in a hotel and matters had gone much further than he had expected because it was a winter night and his former wife's apartment was poorly heated by her infamous landlord.

If anyone thinks I am being frivolous or just talking through my hat on this subject, they are wrong. I have studied it very carefully, from the point of view of immediate personal experience, from the judicious and calm point of view of an observer concerned about the vicissitudes of his friends' marriages, and have taken what I think I may say without immodesty is a scholarly approach. As to personal experience, that is one thing, but what I really take a great deal of pride in is my learning on the subject of marriage. I am not thinking only of all the motion pictures and plays and novels to which I have devoted myself and which for the most part circled about the question of marriage, whether it was *Anna Karenina, Oedipus Rex, Gone With the Wind, Tobacco Road,* or *Abie's Irish Rose.* I am also thinking of what has happened to The Book of Common Prayer, a work which is very influential indeed and in the English-speaking world provides the model for all marriage ceremonies, for even if you are not a communicant of a church which uses The Book of Common Prayer, it is extremely unlikely that you do not go to the motion pictures where, needless to say, you must have encountered the use of the Anglican marriage service more than once and found it very beautiful.

It is very beautiful. But it has been tampered with, and in an unfortunate way, by prudes, I suspect, who have no real feeling for the sacrament of marriage or the beauty of human relationships.

Thus nowadays, at the moment when the groom places the ring upon the bride's hand, the fair bride says: "With this ring I thee wed, with my body I thee worship, with all my worldly goods I thee endow."

How that phrase, "with my body I thee worship," survived, amid other expurgations, is a perplexing matter: probably carelessness. For just look what has happened elsewhere. At a previous moment in the ceremony, the minister asks the bride the following familiar question: "Wilt thou have this man to thy wedded husband, to live together after God's holy ordinance in the holy estate of matrimony? Wilt thou obey him, and serve him, love, honour, and keep him in sickness and in health; and forsaking all others, keep thee only unto him, so long as ye both shall live?" Nowadays, the bride just says that she will do all these things. In the old days before the ceremony was revised, the bride used to have to say: "I take thee to my weddyd husbonde to haue and to holde fro thys day for bether, for wurs, for richer, for porer, in sykeness and hin elthe to be bonour and buxom in bed and at bort tyll deth do us departe yf holy chyrche wol it ordeyne: and ther to I plyche te my throute."

Now this is certainly a far cry from what is pledged today. My edition of The Book of Common Prayer has a commentary in it written by some Victorian named Blunt (God save the mark!) in 1883 and he shows that he is quite disturbed by the old form of the ceremony, even though it was by then long since not in style. He explains that "Bonour and buxom" are the representatives of "Bonnaire," gentle (as in *debonaire*) and "Boughsome," obedient. But that's just silly, as you can see if you look again and regard the context. The bride says that she is going to be bonour and buxom in bed and at board. How can you be gentle at board? Perhaps the pious Victorian is thinking of good manners at the dinner table, but it is not very likely that that's what the authors of the ceremony were thinking about because they had a very different idea of good manners. And for that matter to be obedient in bed does not strike me as being a very cogent promise, though being buxom and *débonair* seems quite sensible, but I don't want to go into unnecessary detail. My main point is that this illustrates how people have not been paying the proper attention to marriage, and how the institution as a whole is in a parlous state, just as is this profound and beautiful ceremony, which has been spoiled by revision, weakened, and ( I believe it is not too much to say ) emasculated.

This brings us back to the Princess Elizabeth. If she is really concerned about matrimony today, let her consider these facts and in particular the degradation of the marriage ceremony. One of these days she will be the secular head of the Church of England, and it will then be possible for her to do something about the whole affair in this very important matter of what is said at the very start of the marriage by the bride to the groom in the presence of witness, friends, and relatives. Who knows what may not come of this?

POSTSCRIPT: A friend of mine married his true love recently, after an arduous courtship full of much misunderstanding. He and his beautiful bride embraced matrimony only after both had often visited psychoanalysts who helped them to understand themselves and each other. The joyous pair sent me the following wedding card:

*Dr. Martin Green & Dr. Theodore Burns*
*announce the marriage of their well-meaning patients*
*Miss Isabel Basel Doolittle & Mr. Bertram Y. Kennedy*

Love is no longer blind! It's a wise man who knows his wife or for that matter himself:

*Ah, Psyche from the regions which*
*Are Holy Land!*

Come live with me and be my wife,
We'll seek the peaks and pits of life
And run the gauntlet of the heart
On mountains or the depths of art.
                    We'll do the most that thinking can
                    Against emotion's Ghenghis Khan.
And we will play on Hallowe'en
Like all souls on the silver screen,
Or at a masked ball ask for fun
Dancing dressed as monk and nun.
                    We'll ride a solemn music's boat
                    When humors cough in breast and throat.
When snow comes like a sailing fleet
We'll skate a ballet in the street,
Though poor as saints or rocks, immense
Our chatter's rich irreverence.
                    And sometimes speak of endless death
                    To quicken every conscious breath.
If one becomes too serious,
The other can bring down the house
With jokes which seem hilarious
About the self's pretentious Ows.
                    I'll be your room-mate and your hoax,
                    The scapeghost of your gentle jokes.
Like Molière's bourgeois gentleman,
You may discover you have been
Speaking blank verse all your life,
And hence you must become my wife.
                    For you will know of metaphors,
                    If I say aeroplanes are bores.

If these excursions seem to you
Interesting as a rendezvous,
             Rich as cake and revenue,
             Handsome as hope and as untrue,
             And full of travel's points of view,
             Vivid as red and fresh as dew,
Come live with me and try my life,
And be my night, my warmth, my wife.

## FUN WITH THE FAMOUS, STUNNED BY THE STARS

*Fame corrupts, absolute fame corrupts
absolutely, all great men are insane.*

It has been my good fortune to meet great men now and then, and these encounters have been very rewarding, so I would like to crash the gate of posterity by hitching my wagon to these stars even if I have to mix metaphors and expose the extent to which I suffer from hero-worship.

One of these great men was a celebrated metaphysician who told me that he was always very polite to other great metaphysicians in print, but did not really think they were very bright because if he did, he would have to stop thinking well of his own system of philosophy, which was not theirs. He chortled when he said this, and this habit is, I think, characteristic of great men: they tend to chortle.

Another great man was a famous poet and the first time I met him, he was visiting a mutual friend and his wife, and he had a new dog, and he was making unkind remarks about editors and critics. This caused an awkward silence because several of the critics were friends of his host and his host was a very kind man who did not like to think ill of anyone. This famous poet kept us all up until four o'clock in the morning with his cynical and dismaying stories, but what's the use of being a great poet if you can't do as you please and stay up late? The second time I met this truly great author was at a cocktail party for a poet who was not very good, not yet, anyway. The great author was standing nervously to one side, and looking as he felt: neglected. I went to talk to him with the lady friend who had come with me, and he said that he had just written a new poem, but he was afraid to recite it to me because of the female element in his audience. She assured him she would not be offended, and she had in fact read everything from Aristophanes and Boccaccio to Henry Miller, John O'Hara and that unjustly suppressed example of eighteenth-century prose, "The Memoirs of Fanny Hill." So the great poet recited his new poem, smirking:

> *Mary had a little lamb,*
>     *His name was Jesus Christ,*
> *God, not Joseph, was her ram,*
>     *But Joseph took it nicet.*

We listeners were offended, not by the reference to sexual intercourse but by the lack of religious understanding and the appalling rhyme.

This disturbed our celebrity who thought that we had reasons which were not literary nor theological for being nervous and distressed. He spoke then of the poet for whom this cocktail party was being given and who was standing about four feet away.

"Do you think he is any good?" said the great poet. "I can't stand his work, but he sends it to me for criticism all the time."

I murmured back in a low voice, alarmed that the subject under discussion might overhear this opinion of his gifts.

"I ought not to go to these parties," said the great poet, "I talk too much."

We said something senseless in reply. Then another poet came to greet the great one and the two exchanged greetings which would have pleased Machiavelli, Metternich and Richelieu. They both explained that they had not read any of the other's works for the past ten years, but had heard other people whom they respected very much speak with no little admiration about these works.

Then the other poet departed to get a new Martini and left us to the mercy of the great poet again.

"What happened to that fellow?" the great poet asked me. "He used to be very gifted and I thought he would turn out well, but somehow he has just petered out. Do you think it was woman trouble? Or does he drink too much?"

I answered that I did not know much about him, fearful again that what was said would be overheard and feeling in all truth that I did not know anything much about anything anyhow.

This incident made me feel that to be a great poet was a mixed blessing at best, if that was the most serene, self-controlled, and Olympian one could be after many years of absolute success. And I also felt that I had better avoid these famous poets because they destroyed my literary illusions and social poise.

So when another famous poet, almost as famous as the previous one, said in a letter about other matters that he was going to be in town and hoped to meet me at last (the *at last* was because I had written to him and about him now and then for ten years) I was pleased but disturbed. I did not really want to meet him. I admired him too much, and was doing very well and did not want to take any unnecessary chances. So far as I was concerned, his work was sufficient for me by way of acquaintance.

First thing you know, I am going down the street and there is this great poet walking toward me. I recognized him by his photographs. He had arrived in town and he must have been on his way, I guess, to a luncheon engagement. Meanwhile I had planned to leave town that night for a hard-earned vacation, so I felt that I ought to say something to him, introduce myself, and explain that I was going out of town, but was very pleased to make his acquaintance.

As I thought of saying this, the great poet passed me. I turned and looked at him and decided to follow him and introduce myself to him as a matter of courtesy. But as I followed him, I wondered what I could possibly say to him? The first thing that came into my head was that I am very glad to meet you and your work has been deteriorating for the past fifteen years.

This did not seem the proper beginning and suggested that I had been warped by being forced to earn my living as a literary critic, but anyway I could not think of anything else to say to him.

Then it occurred to me that the right thing to do would be to ask him to my house for a drink. Before he arrived I would fortify myself with small talk, which I detest, and hard liquor, which I adore because it has often helped me to engage in small talk, and relaxed persiflage, which I like very much.

I had heard that the great poet was on the wagon, but that was beside the point, I was the one who would do the social drinking.

Meanwhile the great poet seemed to have become aware that he was being followed, for he paused, stopped, looked at me as if to say what is all this about? I stopped too and made believe that I was waiting for someone. I was getting ready to speak to him politely and invite him to the house for a drink that afternoon when I remembered that the electric icebox had broken down, so there were no ice cubes.

That settled it. I turned about and went away and left the great poet in peace. It is perfectly true that I could have bought some ice but at the moment what I needed was an excuse and that was the excuse I needed.

❖   ❖   ❖

Since that time, I have reflected upon the nature of this strange encounter. The great poet in question was a very shy man and yet a very worldly one, and one who in addition to becoming a great poet had tried very hard all his life to be a good human being. Perhaps some sense of this goodness made me afraid to meet him, for though shy, I have not tried very hard to be good. But this is idle speculation, it is true, and several other theories come to mind, for example that my admiration for this author was so great that I could no more bear to converse with him than to look into the dazzling sun. Certainly he was not at all like the other great authors I had conversed with, four in number, and I had no reason to think that he had anything but a mildly friendly feeling toward me, though obviously he did not care whether he saw me or not, and anyway many other people were overjoyed to entertain him.

What then can the reason be? or reasons? I was not brought up very well and subsequent events have not tended, for the most part, to make me at ease either with the great or even with those who are not great. Yet I do manage to survive various encounters without irreparable damage on either side, so maybe there was something special here.

This is one extreme. At the other extreme are my encounters with another great poet, a friend of the first great poet and an admirer of the second, and a wonderful man too, shy, original, idiosyncratic, eccentric but at the same time what we might call, very concentric, that is to say, a man who makes it a point of honor to do what is expected of him by other people. Be that as it may, and I am basing these remarks on scattered impressions, I never have any trouble in talking to him, except sometimes it is a question of getting in a word edgewise. But he is usually talking about me and my welfare, which is one reason that he does not like to be interrupted. One time, for example, he had just found out that my lordly salary was fifty-two dollars a week and he was very much upset to hear this, and he tried to explain to me how I could make a great deal more money doing hardly any work at all. But the story of our evenings deserves a special account, I think, and what I want to bring out here was that I had told him about what happened when I did not go up and say hello to the other great poet, and and he was very interested, and he said that he would probably have felt and acted just as I did. The news depressed me, so I asked the waiter for a double Martini (this great man drinks only gin and he does not like anyone else to drink anything else in his company and it was when he learned that I liked gin very much that he concluded that I had good taste and knew how to live), and he asked for a double Martini too, and before long we were reciting to each other just like a barber shop quartet:

> *'In the beginning was the word,'*
> *Superfetation of* τὸ ἕν —

"Very witty, very witty," said my drinking companion, "perhaps one of the most brilliant remarks about life, love, language, and the Incarnation that has ever been uttered."

It was time for him to go to Grand Central Station, so we started out, chanting in antiphony to the disregard of one and all.

"Poetry is like electric light," I remarked as he went through the gates, "good at night, dismal in the daytime. Truly we are fortunate."

"Stick to gin and regular meters," he cried to me as he gave the redcap his suitcases and walked away, resembling Jupiter on his way home to Juno.

"Give me enough hope and I'll hang myself," I said by way of farewell.

For thirty years what madness I have known;
Of solitude the blankness and *longueurs,*
The nervous doubt which thought and art assure,
Causeless despair, or causeless joy alone.

But when I thought of the masters of the heart,
And of the mind and of life's long disease,
And the majesty and fury of great art,
I was renewed like April's wooden trees,

And I was *parvenu* and green with hope.
They pacified the underworld in me:
—What are we? what are we not? when touched by them—
And I rehearsed their passion's history.

His senses great palms stormed by fury,
Keats left for Italy to burn away.
Emerson lived in Eden's innocence,
Thinking the world was like a summer's day.

He did not understand Hawthorne's dark works,
His endless guilt, his passion for the snow.
Mozart knew comedy's great melancholy,
And spoke of Thermidor in Figaro.

The glib, the clever, the fluent, and the vain
Pompom chrysanthemums like Oscar Wilde
Destroyed themselves in witty drawing rooms,
By earnestness and epigrams defiled.

Hugo in Jersey like a sunset shone.
Baudelaire slumped in a deadly tiredness
And saw his own face in the tragic play
Of Poe's face which like drowned Ophelia lay.

Emily Brontë gazed awestruck to see
Passion consume her brother on the moor.
Emily Dickinson went to Washington,
Falling in love like flowers to the floor.

She learned, like heroines in Henry James,
Renunciation like a tower remains
Of Christ's great castle in the Western heart.
And sang. And made a notebook of her art.

Wordsworth on walking tours found innocence,
Harked to the mariner who talked all night
Of the real world, pure consciousness as such,
As if he understood the world of light.

The poet Dostoevsky cried and sang
Of penitence, since he was criminal,
And of forgiveness, wishing to be forgiven
The crime of making love to a little girl.

These masters used their lives like Christmas trees,
They skinned themselves alive to find the truth,
They gazed upon their vileness like excrement.
They ate their hearts to sate the need for love.
They fingered every coiled snake of the mind,
Searching for choice and chance and wish and memory.

They stood upon their heads. They thrust their hands
In furnaces to find what they could bear.
They climbed down pits and wells, and praised
The wilderness, the future, and the truth.
And in the end their separated heads
Glared from a plate and criticized this life!

Don Giovanni, the much-publicized Spanish sportsman, playboy, man about town, loose liver, and singer has been dealt with extensively and comprehensively by such experts as Mozart, Da Ponte, Balzac, George Byron, George Bernard Shaw, and other deep thinkers.

So it would just be gilding the lily, carrying coals to Newcastle, and really redundant to rehearse the whole business of his life and works once more, except that in some respects these profound commentators seem to have missed the point. Perhaps this was because they did not have the benefit of the Kinsey Report's confusions. Most of these authors seem to be under the impression, for example, that Giovanni is having himself a wonderful time until the very end when he gets pulled down to hell screaming at the top of his voice. Before that, practically everything was fun, fun, fun.

But this is quite untrue.

He was unhappy from the very start and at the peak of his career, too. I am not speaking of the difficulty of some of his affairs of the heart, or the chancy risks he ran. The real point is that promiscuity is undiscriminating as well as indiscriminate, and Giovanni kept running against the stone wall of this fact.

Take, for example, some of his conversations with his aide-de-camp, Leporello, to whom he was wont to brag about his conquests, naturally. There was the time that he met a very beautiful girl named Alice, and in about two hours she came running across the room to him, saying: "I am going to love the pants off you!" Naturally he was delighted with Alice at the moment, and when he went home he told Leporello about her highly charged remark, and about how Alice kept a chocolate bar next to her bed at night in case she woke up because she wanted every moment to be jammed with sweetness. Naturally this made Leporello's mouth water, and he hoped that Giovanni would settle down for a while, for Alice seemed to require a good deal of attention and energy. Nothing of the kind. And Leporello should have known better. Alice told Giovanni he had to marry her or beat it, and he became very angry and told her that she was not that important to him, so that was the end of that.

Another interesting time was when Giovanni and Leporello discussed rape with a girl named Florence, who was a friend of theirs. Giovanni maintained that there was no such thing as rape, short of violence, and he inquired as to why a girl who was attacked did not kick the rude, impetuous, and unfortunate amorist in the testicles, which would certainly give him pause. "Oh, no nice girl would do that," said Florence shyly. The fact that Giovanni did not appreciate the nobility of this reply shows how little he understood women. And as Phyllis, a friend of both Giovanni and Florence, once said pensively to Florence: "All men are bastards. But some bastards are nice." Here again I think it is clear that Giovanni did not grasp the true uniqueness and profound insight of some of the girls he knew. And the reason for this blindness is that promiscuity is like the dark in that it makes all cats look gray.

The best example of how Giovanni was mixed up about what he wanted is his affair with a girl named Marlene, who was really something, partly because she seemed to be very quiet, refined, and studious. Giovanni as usual had to talk it all over with Leporello, and he told Leporello that Marlene was breaking all records. He was referring to a broad joke of which the two were very fond, and which sometimes is formulated as follows: a Frenchman says there are seventy-seven ways to make love and an amazed American says that there is just one way in America. "Comment?" asks the Frenchman. "Well, er," stammers the bashful American, "the gentleman gets on top of the lady." "Soixante-dix-huit," says the delighted Frenchman.

Well, after meeting Marlene, Giovanni kept telling Leporello how wonderful she was, and first he said sixty-nine, and then seventy-nine, and then eighty-four, ninety-six, and then one hundred and twenty-two, one hundred and forty, six hundred and fifty-one, and finally he announced that he had lost count, which of course left poor Leporello gasping like an exhausted marathon runner.

Leporello thought that anyway this time curiosity and a desire to break the world's record might keep Giovanni fixed on Marlene for a while. He was wrong again. Marlene and Giovanni had a big fight and the supposed reason was that Marlene said that Giovanni was neither flirtatious nor affectionate enough. Giovanni replied heatedly that there was a time for everything, and just as no one would expect an adult man to wear diapers, so no real lady would expect flirtation and affection every time there was any question of making love, and long after a basic understanding had been achieved. So Marlene threw him out of the house, and the irritated Giovanni told Leporello he was glad because he was getting bored with the same torso all the time.

Now the question has often been raised as to why Giovanni was like that, why he was so full of unrest, never really satisfied, always eager to make love to more and more girls, and particularly to other men's wives?

Various hypotheses have been suggested, and smirked about. It is believed by some of the latest students of the subject that Giovanni really wanted to make love to his mother and no girl ever satisfied him because of course no girl was his mother. A subtle refinement of this interpretation explains that the reason he had to go after other fellows' girls and wives is that during infancy and childhood his father was always taking his mother away from him and locking the door, so this incessant and excessive adultery was, in fact, a long revenge upon his father, and the entire male sex because his mother had preferred husband to son. Then again it is said that Giovanni found every girl to be just like his mother once he knew her, though he always hoped to find one who would be unlike mother, so he had to run away from all of them because incest is wrong. And also there is the implausible idea that Giovanni did not like girls at all, that's why he was never satisfied with any one of them, and though this theory may seem far-fetched because of the inordinate attention Giovanni paid to the girls, lots of truths are far-fetched, like the discovery of America, for instance.

It is certainly true that Giovanni enjoyed and was much more excited by the process of courting and seducing a girl than he was excited by any actual physical reality and gratification. And it is true too that each conquest made his ego feel better, and this would also explain why he liked other men's girls. And he was undoubtedly a hit-and-run driver;

once he made the girl, he was likely to beat it. All of these theories may or may not be true, but after one has reviewed all of them and weighed them critically, there is only one conclusion one can feel any certainty about, namely, that Giovanni was a Lesbian, that is to say, someone who likes to sleep with girls.

From him to me what services,
Clipping the mussed hair on my head,
— He does not know how near he is
To what is under, living or dead.
Sir, in my mind there is a need
To know your intimate profession,
Figaro! not the fattest weed
On Lethe's bank in endless session

Knows more than I monotony's
Gungray and endless empty cars!
But what are your immediacies
Amid the thick and curl of hairs?
Now, through horn-rimmed glasses, you
Blink and look straight ahead of me
To what warm coast of brilliant blue?
(O tourist mind of revery!)

How shall we come to terms at last
And talk like friends with ease and poise?
All men are strangers dark and lost,
All are deceived as girls and boys.
There is a gulf which I detest
Between the self that clips my hair
And the warm beasts lounging in my head
Where past and present soil the air!

Othello was a very gifted Moorish soldier who had been hired by the Venetian government to command its troops against any foreign powers that had a desire to interfere with the very profitable overseas trade of Venice. Same as ever, things don't really change.

Othello was regarded by the lords of Venice as a military genius and it was also felt by all that he was a very brave man. It was natural that the Venetian nobility should invite him to dinner and enjoy hearing stories of his experiences overseas and in strange parts of the world. Senator Brabantio invited General Othello to dinner so often that his beautiful daughter Desdemona (beautiful in character as well as from a physical standpoint) fell in love with the successful soldier.

Now in spite of all his military victories and other gratifying things in his life, Othello felt that there was something about him which made him not quite as good as the Venetian nobility. He was dark-skinned and they were on the pale side, though somewhat olive-skinned; but also it was a matter of Othello's not being well-bred or at ease in social situations the way that a Venetian gentleman would be. Given this feeling about himself, Othello was unable to perceive that Desdemona had fallen in love with him. He thought she was just interested in military strategy when she listened to the stories of his adventures, with the passion and absorption of one of those Brooklyn Dodger fans, watching the Dodgers in a crucial series against the St. Louis Cardinals.

Desdemona certainly did like Othello's stories and she admired his courage and masculinity, and perhaps she fell in love with him also because he was very strong and did not resemble her father in the least. Anyway, she was infatuated with him, and he did not have the least inkling of her feelings, and in the end Desdemona had to resort to what was a pretty cute trick, she had to tell Othello that if he had a friend who was just like him in every respect, would he please bring him to call because she would probably fall in love with him!

Othello finally took this hint which was as much of a hint as a five-o'clock steam whistle. He was overjoyed. He knew very well that the

Senator would not like the prospect of such a marriage, and this may have intensified his feelings, but the couple decided to elope and they did, and everyone else, including a former suitor of Desdemona named Rollo, rejected but still quite hopeful, was very upset.

It goes without saying, human nature being what it fears, if deprived of love's fulfillment, that there was a great deal of excitement. Rollo was working hand in hand with a son of a bitch named Iago who was one of Othello's officers and did not like his superior. The two of them, Iago and Rollo, woke up the Senator in the middle of the night, right after they heard about the elopement, and in no time at all, the Senator was calling up his friends and asking that the marriage be annulled.

The clever Iago, who knew very well how to hurt people's feelings, yelled up anonymously at the Senator's window this lascivious outcry:

"A black man (ram) is tupping (on top of and having sexual intercourse with) your pure white ewe (daughter, mother, sister, virgin, and wife) (and you)," he cried at the top of his voice.

This had the expected effect on the father, and he convened the entire Venetian government at about three o'clock in the morning and demanded that they put Othello in the clink. He said that Othello must have used drugs because no well-bred Venetian girl in her right mind would marry a foreigner like that. Desdemona and Othello were summoned from the nuptial bed of their wedding night and they explained what had happened clearly and calmly, though Othello did get a little excited. The Venetian nobility were pretty much convinced, particularly by Desdemona's girlish and touching and very authentic-seeming account of what had occurred, and they thought that in any case there was no use in crying over spilt milk, what was done was done, they might as well make the best of things, especially since, as is normal, war was imminent, and Othello was a very valuable man, and they had to think of the good of the community and their investments.

The Senator was not appeased, however, and he refused to get adjusted to the inevitable like a sensible man, for his primal feelings were involved; it was as if someone had insulted his mother's honor, he had been punched in the nose of his psyche, he felt that nothing could console him, and he made one parting remark which stayed in Othello's mind and injured it the way ground glass will injure the stomach. He said to Othello that the girl had betrayed her father and would betray him, too, for a girl's attitude toward her father was the basis of the emotional pattern and behavior she brought to her husband. This shows what a handy weapon a little inexpensive and trite and false psychologizing can be.

We come now to Iago, who was really nasty, for he saw in this marriage a chance to do a great deal of harm. He disliked Othello very much, but it is not clear just why he did. He *thought* he had good reasons for disliking him and it may have seemed that he did not have good reasons, but I don't think this prevalent impression is true because Iago was always trying to find reasons for hating and harming Othello and he was jumping from one reason to another in an effort to convince himself. The first reason was that Othello had appointed another fellow, Cassio, to be his second in command in the army, instead of giving this position to Iago who was, it can be said with reasonable certainty, superior to Cassio in knowledge and experience. But that kind of thing is always happening. And this reason for hating Othello was not very convincing really, although Iago communicated it to his friend Rollo right after Desdemona's marriage, when Rollo was in a rage and attacked Iago for permitting it to happen, as if he could have done anything about it. But Rollo was a dreadful dumb-bell, whom Iago himself had described as just poor white trash.

Now this first reason disappeared when Iago managed to get the pleasure-loving Cassio very drunk, as a result of which he was dismissed by Othello and replaced by Iago. It might be thought that this is just a superficial view for if Iago's feelings had once been very hurt, he might have remained full of hatred for Othello, even if he was afterward given what he wanted in the first place. But the fact is that Othello and Iago had become very close friends and Othello hardly did anything but praise Iago and speak warmly to him and call him honest, honest Iago, a wonderful guy.

Iago had a third reason too, for he was, as has been pointed out, desperately in quest of reasons which would justify the hatred he felt toward Othello. This third reason was his suspicion that Othello had made love successfully to Iago's wife Emilia. But it is not a very good reason either, it did not convince Iago in the least, and it is perfectly clear that he was not behaving like a jealous husband; for example, compare his behavior with the way in which Othello responded to the idea that Desdemona might have been unfaithful to him. Moreover, Iago did not act as if he cared very much about Emilia, he showed no signs whatever of affection, and one might even go so far as to say that he did not particularly like girls, he was too preoccupied with making the worst of his talent for evil and the destruction of human relationships. In fact, he was a virtuoso of evil and used his knowledge of the human heart the way a great violinist uses a Stradivarius. He certainly did like money very much and this too was so strong a preoccupation that it also suggests that he was the kind of person who does not love anyone, not even himself.

Iago was looking for reasons for justifying his hatred of Othello because he was making all sorts of subtle imputations about Desdemona, telling Othello that he did not know what to make of it but Cassio had certainly been behaving in a very friendly way toward Desdemona. The details are not important. Othello was finally convinced that his wife had slept with Cassio, he accused her, gave her no serious chance to acquit herself, choked her to death, and it all ended with Iago's treacherous destructiveness discovered, Othello brought to his senses, and committing suicide. Iago was punished, but what good did that do Othello or Desdemona?

The important thing is that Iago had no good reason for hating Othello the way he did. This is what one finds truly horrifying, though I know well enough that it goes on all the time. Iago was just evil the way that dogs bark, the sun shines, burrs stick, cats meow, and lightning strikes. Consequently poor Desdemona was dead in early youth, and for no good reason.

Now there has been some argument about whether Iago did have a good reason for hating Othello, a good reason in the sense that Othello

**45**

would have had a good reason for hating Cassio, if Cassio had made love to Desdemona with her great enthusiasm, applause, and cooperation. That's what one might call a good reason. A studious fellow named Kittredge thinks that Iago did have several good reasons and takes Iago's own declarations and avowals at what is practically their face-value, which was the way Othello made such a fool of himself. On the other hand, S. T. Coleridge, an expert on German philosophy, indecision, and laudanum, speaks of one of Iago's soliloquies as "the motive-hunting of a motiveless malignity." And the latter is proven right, I think, if we examine the background. Shakespeare, the brilliant country boy who wrote the Broadway hit on which this adaptation has been based, took the story from an Italian best-seller called the "Hecatommithi," by a fellow named Giovanni Battista Giraldi. Now in this short novel, which is not very good, Iago has a perfectly good reason for hating Othello: *he is a rejected suitor.* As I see it, this is conclusive: Shakespeare took the story by Giraldi and changed it when it suited his purpose. He had a perfectly good motive at hand for Iago and he omitted it, replacing it with half-hearted efforts to find motives.

Shakespeare must have known a thing or two about motives because he seems to think that the worst thing of all is not to have motives. That's what was wrong with Iago and that is what is meant when it is said that he was really a villain, a being who does evil for its own sake.

I wonder what happened to Shakespeare or his friends, or both, to make him think of these things. Perhaps he disliked his own suspicious nature, or perhaps he did not like a world in which the innocent are unjustly choked to death, like Desdemona. He must have been a very unhappy man, even though very talented.

He seems to be saying that all he can say is that Desdemona is in her grave.

The starlight's intuitions pierced the twelve,
The brittle night sky sparkled like a tune
Tinkled and tapped out on the xylophone.
Empty and vain, a glittering dune, the moon
Arose too big, and, in the mood which ruled,
Seemed like a useless beauty in a pit;
And then one said, after he carefully spat:
"No matter what we do, he looks at it!

"I cannot see a child or find a girl
Beyond his smile which glows like that spring moon."
"—Nothing no more the same," the second said,
"Though all may be forgiven, never quite healed
The wound I bear as witness, standing by;
No ceremony surely appropriate,
Nor secret love, escape or sleep because
No matter what I do, he looks at it—"

"Now," said the third, "no thing will be the same:
I am as one who never shuts his eyes,
The sea and sky no more are marvelous,
And I no longer understand surprise!"
"Now," said the fourth, "nothing will be enough,
—I heard his voice accomplishing all wit:
No word can be unsaid, no deed withdrawn,
—No matter what is said, he measures it!"

"Vision, imagination, hope or dream,
   Believed, denied, the scene we wished to see?
   It does not matter in the least: for what
   Is altered, if it is not true? That we
   Saw goodness, as it is — *this* is the awe
   And the abyss which we will not forget,
   His story now the sky which holds all thought:
   No matter what I think, I think of it!"

"And I will never be what once I was,"
   Said one for long as narrow as a knife,
"And we will never be what once we were;
   We have died once; this is a second life."
"My mind is spilled in moral chaos," one
   Righteous as Job exclaimed, "now infinite
   Suspicion of my heart stems what I will,
   —No matter what I choose, he stares at it!"

"I am as one native in summer places
   —Ten weeks' excitement paid for by the rich;
   Debauched by that and then all winter bored,
   The sixth declared, "His peak left us a ditch!"
"He came to make this life more difficult,"
   The seventh said, "No one will ever fit
   His measure's heights, all is inadequate:
   No matter what I do, what good is it?"

"He gave forgiveness to us: what a gift!"
The eighth chimed in. "But now we know how much
Must be forgiven. But if forgiven, what?
The crime which was will be; and the least touch
Revives the memory: what is forgiveness worth?"
The ninth spoke thus: "Who now will ever sit
At ease in Zion at the Easter feast?
No matter what the place, he touches it!"

"And I will always stammer, since he spoke,"
One, who had been most eloquent, said, stammering.
"I looked too long at the sun; like too much light,
So too much goodness is a boomerang,"
Laughed the eleventh of the troop. "I must
Try what he tried: I saw the infinite
Who walked the lake and raised the hopeless dead:
No matter what the feat, he first accomplished it!"

So spoke the twelfth; and then the twelve in chorus:
"Unspeakable unnatural goodness is
Risen and shines, and never will ignore us;
He glows forever in all consciousness;
Forgiveness, love, and hope possess the pit,
And bring our endless guilt, like shadow's bars:
No matter what we do, he stares at it!
What pity then deny? what debt defer?
We know he looks at us like all the stars,
And we shall never be as once we were,
This life will never be what once it was!"

# III

## THE TRUE, THE GOOD, AND THE BEAUTIFUL

Dear Citizens,
I heard the newsboys shouting "Europe! Europe!"
It was late afternoon, a winter's day
Long as a prairie, wool and ashen gray,
And then I heard the silence, drop by drop,
And knew I must again confront myself:
"What shall I cry from my window?" I asked myself,
"What shall I say to the citizens below?
Since I have been a *privileged character*
These four years past. Since I have been excused
From the war for the lesser evil, merciless
As the years to girls who once were beautiful.
What have I done which is a little good?
What apples have I grasped, for all my years?
What starlight have I glimpsed for all my guilt?"

Then to the dead silence I said, in hope:
"I am a student of the morning light,
And of the evil native to the heart.
I am a pupil of emotion's wrongs
Performed upon the glory of this world.
Myself I dedicated long ago
—Or prostituted, shall I say?—to poetry,
The true, the good, and the beautiful,
Infinite fountains inexhaustible,
Full as the sea, old as the rocks,
                    new as the breaking surf —"

## THE SILENCE ANSWERED HIM ACCUSINGLY

"Don't fool yourself," the silence said to me,
"Don't tell yourself a noble lie once more!"

Then to the silence, being accused, I said:
"I teach the boys and the girls in my ageing youth,
I try to tell them the little I know of truth,
Saying, In the beginning is the word,
And in the end and everywhere in love,
In all love's places and in the mind of God.
Three words I speak, though they are bare and far,
                              untouchable as a star,
*The true, the good, and the beautiful,*
Shifting my tones as if I said to them
*Candy, soda, fruits and flowers,*
And if they hear, what thunderclap uproars,
                              unanimous applause,
(Extremely gratifying signs of pleasure).

'Behold the unspeakable beauty,' I say to them,
'Arise and lift your eyes and raise your hearts
In celebration and in praise because
Plato's starlight glitters amid the shocking wars.'"

"What empty rhetoric," the silence said,
"You teach the boys and girls that you may gain
The bread and wine which sensuality
Sues like a premier or a president.
These are illusions of your sense of guilt
Which shames you like a vain lie when revealed.
The other boys slumped like sacks on desperate shores."

"But well you know the life which I have lived,
Cut off, in truth, by all that I have been
From the normal pleasures of the citizen.
How often in the midnight street I passed
The party where the tin horns blew contempt
And the rich laughter rose as midnight struck,
The party where the New Year popped and foamed,
Opening like champagne or love's wet crush,
The while I studied long the art which in
America wins silence like a wall.
—I am a student of the kinds of light,
I am a poet of the wakeful night,
In new and yet unknown America.
I am a student of love's long defeat.
I gave the boys and girls my mind and art,
I taught them of the early morning light:
May I not cite this as a little good?"

# SOME PRESENT THINGS ARE CAUSES OF TRUE FEAR

Dear Citizens,
Some say this age is hardly worth a sneer,
Yet let us applaud and cheer for certain things,
Let us not use the mind merely to jeer.

Come, let us praise the noble lies which were
To justify the millions dead in war.

Does not the honor of man appear in this,
He must deceive himself in waking consciousness?
He must have reasons noble as Jesus Christ,

Chanted like anthems in great stadiums,
Sung to Justice, Hope, and Charity,
Crusades, charades, parades, and masquerades
To guard democracy or hypocrisy.

And if the gold rush is the true career,
And if the economy has made it clear
How manic depressive Uncle Sam must be,
This metaphor is mere analogy.

Yet let us praise the noble sentiment:
That every poor boy can be president.

Come, let us praise the life in which we live
(*Pretend no more that happiness does not exist!*).
Have we not television and Broadway,
Victrolas, coca-colas, powerful cars?

And every principality and power
Which gives dominion in the earth and air?
Balloons, buffoons, crooners, and fine cartoons,
While every boy can be a millionaire?

When Tin Pan Alley formulates the heart,
When Hollywood fulfills the laws of dream,
When the radio is poet laureate
To Heinz, Palmolive, Swift, and Chevrolet,

(Eloquent operas soaring night and day!)
*Pretend no more that happiness does not exist.*
Let us not be embittered, citizens,
Because the beau ideal once glittered for us.

And if some students of the age declare:
"As for this age, it's hardly worth a jeer,
Hitler and Stalin rule our ruthless time,
This is the age of matchless worldwide crime!"

Let these romantic critics go elsewhere,
*Elsewhere pretend that happiness is not like this.*

Do we not have, in fine, depression and war
Certain each generation? Who would want more?
O what unsated heart would ask for more?

# LUNAS ARE TEMPTING TO OLD CONSCIOUSNESS

Dear Citizens,
You are a summer people, all year long,
The seashore is the lyric of your lives,
And all hearts quicken when the breaker strives
To curve and fall, like love, forever wrong.

The strong rocks also serve the fickled soul,
The sand is rough with goodness like a towel.

Cartoons, come true, run forth in bathing suits
Cheery as flutes, spontaneous as brutes.

The self-enjoyment of the flesh is full,
The nakedness is warm and admirable.


Nevertheless the Luna Park is near,
The roller-coaster soars and dives to fear.

Hark, from the coiling track come screams like jazz,
As if they jumped from brinks of a burning house.
How much some love the gross and plunging shock
As if the screeching broke the block to luck!
Why do they hate their lives?
Why do they wish to die?
Believing in vicious lies,
Afraid to remember and cry.
Nearby in little caves a little train
Seeks mystery and darkness like a vine.
Upon a wheel the couples are revolved,
As if tomorrow's blank had been resolved.

58

Not far, before a door, and with a roar,
A girl's skirt is blown up! showing her hips,
Her drawers, her giggles, her belly and—surprise!
Panic like rape shudders and shakes her eyes.

Soon at the boardwalk sandwiches are rich.
Apples and cones are sticky, licky, lush.
The sated summer people now may look
At abnormality's crude picture book.

Perversity attacks the mind like a storm,
Seeing the fat lady with the gashouse form.
And as the Sunday wanes, and the flesh tires,
How the unconscious stretches, yawns, rises, wanders,
                        aspires and admires!

A Negro's face appears, to grin, if hit,
And hurt by baseballs, sublimation sweet!
Last is the gallery where the guns are neat:
The hearts not satisfied and still denied
Can win a mamma doll with a good shot.

This is the Luna of the heart's desire,
This is the play and park we all admire.

Lo, from the muff of sleep, though darkened, strong,
I rose to read the fresh news of the age:
"Elizabeth would like to be a horse!"
(Though she'll be Queen of England, in due course.)

While in the South Pacific Southern boys
Upon a flagship raised the Stars & Bars
As if the South had won the Civil War.
Meanwhile in Washington Ickes declares

That every plant owned by the government
Should go to G.I.s when they come back home.
—What does he think this is, Utopia?
He should have stood in bed and read a poem.

These politicians have an easy time,
They can say anything, they have no shame,
Kiss babies and blow promises to all
And chant that everything is wonderful.

Awed or indifferent, bemused or ill at ease,
We who are poets play the game which is
A deadly earnest searching of all hearts
As if we struggled with a puzzle's parts,

Making the huge assumption that there is
A lucid picture which these fragments fit,
Disheveled in our clumsy pious hands,
A picture true, good, and appropriate,

Raised up, like Joseph, from the unjust pit.
—And yet suppose that we are wrong? and in all pathos
We handled foolishly essential chaos?
                            What then?
What but with patient hope to try again?

Dear Citizens,
How little we have to say to each other. How much
We have, if we lay bare our hearts,
                    how much, if we
But take away the masks which hide us
From our gaze and fear, tied to the past to the last.
—O Citizens, let us frankly confess
We know our lives are lived by lies.
And, Citizens, let us not be estranged.
Surely the wars will end, there will be peace
                    (A mad world, my masters,
                    A world senseless and cruel),
Goodness will not seem strange as bearded ladies,
Riches will not be wasted by the fool,
And knowlege will not be shabby genteel.
Great works of art will not evoke the jeers
Of those whose ignorance is arrogant,
                    (A sad world, my masters,
                    Yet beautiful, withal).

Grotesque and awkward as the ironclad knights,
An arch-Shakespearean radical recites:
*Duncan is dead, and Desdemona, innocent,*
*Is choked to death. The true, the good,*
*And the beautiful have been struck down*
*Because of what they are. No matter what you say,*
*This is not brushed away. No matter what you say,*
*This is the way it is, year by year and day by day.*

## THE PAST'S GREAT POWER OVERPOWERS EVERY HOUR

Dear Citizens,
We live upon the past and day by day
The past destroys us. Who can look back?
And who can see the back of his head?
And who can see the depths of his mind?
Who can so turn his head upon his neck
That as he runs he holds the past in view?
For who can look both north and south at once?

Come, let us play *cache-cache* or blind-man's bluff,
And pin the tail on the abundant goat
                    for all our guilt,
As if we did not know in blind-man's bluff
And all the arts and all the games each one
But seeks himself? As if you never knew at all
That everywhere you tour, you take yourself.

            When, Citizens,
I placed a seashell to my ear, I heard
My heart roar PANDEMONIUM,
                    which was to say
Every devil from hell yells in your heart,
Or shuffles coarsely as coal rides down a chute.

For is it not, in truth, an obscene play,
The past which senselessly recites in us,
Obsessive as the whippoorwill,
Like starlight on the pane, irrational,
—Inspired by what? inspired by the blaze
Of the true, the good , and the beautiful.

Awake, my dears, and be deceived no more:
What is our hope, except to tell the truth?

# THE **EARLY**
## **MORNING** LIGHT

In the real dark night of the soul, it is
always three o'clock in the morning.

*F. Scott Fitzgerald*

That time of year you may in me behold
When Christmas trees are blazing on the walk,
Raging amid stale snow against the cold
And low sky's bundled wash, senseless as chalk.
Hissing and ravenous the brilliant plant,
Rising like eagerness, a rushing pyre
(As when the *tutti* bursts forth, and the chant
Soars up — hurrahing! — from the Easter choir).

But this is only true at four o'clock,
At noon the fifth year is once more abused,
I bring a distant girl apples and cake,
Pictures, secrets, lastly my swollen heart,
Now boxed and tied by what I know of art
— But as before accepted and refused.

## SHE WAS THE GIRL WITHIN THE PICTURE FRAME

Sometimes the girl on boyhood's silver screen
—The surface makes me nervous as a cat—
Sometimes the girl Vermeer once marveled at,
For there is in her face the famous queen
Who makes all other ladies seem unseen
—Sometimes the Countess in the minuet
By Mozart, hopelessly her laureate,
—Darkling, I hardly know just what I mean.

The expensive suburb has begun to rot.
The latest boys and girls, full of the ache
Of being, are knocking at the gate,
As if a deathless day began to dawn,
Old immortality their natural lot:
—This news is meaningless. For she was born,
Look, in some other world!—and you were not!

## "MY LOVE, MY LOVE, MY LOVE, WHY HAVE YOU LEFT ME ALONE?"

Midmost my twenty-ninth eternity
When hope and expectation sank to ash,
I saw the girl superb in memory,
O far tree! —poplar!—in the lightning flash!
So that, being cowardly, I drank the fire
Which gave the coal-eyed Poe, in Baltimore,
The rocking enraptured sea of his desire,
The death he sang, black handsome nevermore.

Poor Poe! and curséd poets everywhere:
Taught by their strict art to reject the eas-
Y second-best, the well-known lesser good,
They cry exactly to the blank blue air
Love absolute, in the ancient wood
Conscious and scorned like curly Socrates.

## "WHEN YOU SAID HOW YOU'D GIVE ME THE KEYS TO MY HEART"

Once waiting in that studied living room
Joy glittered and was very beautiful
As when a child you looked at vaudeville,
The song and dance man prancing like a groom,
The *savoir-faire* magician, quick as light,
—As if God said: You are again as pure
As numbers, innocence returns once more,
The past forgiven like bad dreams last night.

Your life begins once more, Eden anew!
—Real room, real life, anger and tiredness.
Hope and imagination like the blue
Which Cézanne saw, looking from loneliness:
Far off and cold the sky; and both of us
Accused and recognized by nothingness.

Serene, cool and composed, and easygoing
They think you are because your smiling face
Is still, and generous, and like a growing
Summer, big and rich and luminous.
The furies and the foibles do not show,
The sickness, sorrow, weakness, and the fall,
The heartbreak of the little pensive girl.
How beautiful you are you do not know,

Because you cannot see yourself at all
Because you have been beautiful so long,
—The law and lore of jewels as blind as snow.
It is so long since it was otherwise,
—And I will never be as once I was,
Furious at the crossroads, striking at what I do not know.

# THE SELF-BETRAYAL WHICH IS NOTHING NEW

> There are no second acts in American life.
> *F. Scott Fitzgerald*

Look now, miraculous, *mirabilis*, and true!
The lightning flash or new America
Stumbled on foolishly! what can I do
To make myself most prosperous for her?
I asked myself, conjuring dignities:
Bestseller book or hit upon Broadway,
All of the limelight's bright banalities,
Hurried to Hollywood and a photoplay,

Or a high chair in the old academies?
Lucky or strong, I can get everything
But what I want the most! For having these,
I would be but a matinée's false king,
For in that glare and gilt, I would not be
The one who wants to know her endlessly.

I wish I had a pony or a trot
To read the obscure Latin of your heart,
Falsely I wish I were what I am not,
I would if but I could play any part
(After so many years to come to this!)
—And yet, I know, lost in this empty pass
The very shift and metamorphosis
Would merely bring me to the heart of loss.

For being what I am foists up the wish
—Once lifted from my being's element
I'd gasped with bulging eyes like a hooked fish,
Dumbfounded by my gratified intent:
Behold how in this trope, drawn from the sea,
Two worlds are separated endlessly.

To be with you is sudden happiness,
No matter what hours expectation rose.
It is exciting as early success
After the fears the adolescent knows,
The panicky conceit, the precious pose,
The stagefright at the footlights of the play.
But at your side joy grows as new as May
And like an orchestra the hour flows.

Or I am on a moving, modern boat
Victorious upon the seven seas
From Brooklyn to Hong-Kong. And every thought
Childhood and manhood could not appease
Forgiven in my mind. This is because
You have become my fear and my applause.

## "THERE'LL BE OTHERS BUT NON SO FOR ME"

Some *bon vivant* of the heart might have come for her,
If not for me, sick in all consciousness,
Someone as rich and gay as music is,
And not like me drawn by each straining cur
Ambition and desire loose to the game,
Some being unpossessed and generous.
She would have sung and been spontaneous,
And sauntered in the summer's foam and flame.

Yet from the sadness of what has not been,
Look how there is, above unhappiness,
A certain thing which is not meaningless;
Phoenix affection rises again and again,
Beyond the harm and loss wincing in us:
A bird still chants and is magnanimous.

## "MY LIPS WENT LIVID FOR FROM THE JOY OF FEAR"

Once by the false and rotten river, late
In the September light warm on the lawn,
We lounged all afternoon. But then came fate
As brutal as the day that I was born,
Disguised as two girls who became my luck,
Both Gibson beauties worshipped by a child.
My casual look was thoughtless as we smiled.
And then the image loomed serene and mild.

I wished that I was not my self and died,
Wishing to be the famous Southerner
Who seemed the fitting complement to her,
Is any imagination more infamous?
(After so many years to come to this!)
As if the famous past could be denied!

O Jan Vermeer of Delft, descend, come near
The Hudson and the West's last capital.
Here is the new Ophelia beautiful:
Only your lucid brush could make her clear
And vivid as the daughter of the Swan.
Vermeer, you too!—the early morning light
Only the sleepless see, gazing all night —
Return as faint and delicate as dawn.

Pretty and beautiful, romping and yet
Serene as statues of the classic age,
Her goodness generous in her luminous face,
Through cruel pride rack the world with rage,
Or power and vanity dance their minuet,
Her candor and her gaze are marvelous:
Marvelous shines her candor and her gaze.

And if and when and should because I mean
To fall and dream and fall to seem because I hope
As when a fire's clear furs or fat tongues leap,
A flowing flawless flowering tulip scene:
Although I thought that only peasants sought
For happiness, strict happiness I touch
Because, though trivially, and in the bush
Of idiom's idiot (whom accident hath wrought),

I knew one scene. Let the Americas
Swallow me like a broken bird or toy,
Or come confusions of the Judgment Day,
Annulling that which was a perfect joy,
Because no matter what the cause, or long remorse,
I knew one scene of that romantic play.

Whistles like light in leaves, O light
And starlight on the heights, the reach of speech,
"I like you very much, but not tonight,"
And other true truths which no one can teach
Because emotion is a Christmas tree
Blazing and glaring after the holiday,
Quickly rushing to darkness, falling away,
Hissing like flakes, though sparkling brilliantly.

Evergreen, heart forever! The head afire
Flowing and flowering in a fountain's death
Declares all turns and burns and yet returns,
The breast arises from the falls of breath,
After the burst and lapsing of desire,
Light! Light like the deathless past remains.

Being suspicious of great happiness,
Let us a little while retreat and wait
To understand what freedom amid fate
Remains, for freedom is the sole access
To true desire. Time is most merciless
When generous. And we must hesitate;
Choose tremblingly before the deathless gate,
For this is life: nearby is nothingness.

But nonetheless, the more I think of it,
The more the promise grows, though difficult,
As in the hours when the headfirst child
Shudders amid his mother's mounting fit:
Small pain before the endless joy and guilt
With which the mind and heart will be beguiled.

To give too much and to expect too much
Is Timon's terror or tormenting track.
We of his kind but merely wish to touch,
Hold hands, joyous and generous. What lack
Makes for this drunkenness, spendthrift affection?
Like a scared horse, the heart rears up and neighs,
Running in panic from the least rejection,
And cannot play as a simple fountain plays,

Expecting nothing but to rise and fall,
Since it is false and true to hope at all
For gratitude and love. Yet who can cope
With hope, no matter what cynicism shows,
Precious and vain as adolescent prose.

Now I will have something to think about
Joyously for the rest of endless life.
Meanwhile, to pass the time and not to shout,
I'll think about the time cold as a knife,
And sometimes pause to laugh, or pause in awe,
Because each time I look at her again
Freshly I fall in love with her once more,
And seek new pseudonyms so that my pen

Will not reveal just who is beautiful,
Like a warm animal, yet like a queen,
Beyond my metaphor and parable,
—But this is vain, because, as she is seen,
A dunce will know exactly who I mean,
Lucky as Midas or as pitiful.

## AFTER THE PASSION WHICH MADE ME A FOOL

Not in this life, dark dear and pretty sister;
Not upon Eighth Street where the famous School
Of Paris echoes in colors which the painter
Drew from self-consciousness, a risky jewel;
Not in Vermont, in June, in the gay light,
Near the girl's school, used by the modern dancers;
—This is our junket to the end of the night
Mocked by true questions and by true, false answers.

—Some other life, dark pretty long hurt dear,
Some other world, perhaps, where all who marry
Live with their choice, however strong their fear,
Though like the hunch that hunchbacks carry
All of this life, it is no happiness,
Only the open wound of consciousness.

Some girl serene, some girl whose being is
Affection, and in love with natural things,
In whom the summer like a choir sings,
Yet with a statue's white celebrities
Although the city falls. Golden and sleek,
Spontaneous and strong, quickened and one
To wake for joy, and to bring forth a son
Who climbs with conscious laughter every peak!

But well I know the party rush, the black
Rapids of feeling falling to a bride,
Trapped in the present or the body's lack,
Tall reason's new hat quickly thrown aside,
And soon a child rising and toiling like me
With the dark accidents of strange identity.

## HOW STRANGE TO OTHERS, NATURAL TO ME

Famous infatuation or disease
Has fixed in me until the end of life,
As if a monstrous sister or a wife
Made me a twin tied like the Siamese.
Hence must I wait in patience and in awe,
Knowing that every time I look at it,
No matter the pseudonym or counterfeit,
The same fate draws my passion like a law.

Though I conceal what is so powerful,
And fascinating as a naked queen,
And try all masks to hide from ridicule,
—It is in vain because I will be seen,
No one fools anyone except a fool:
Even the blind will know just what I mean.

Her father's early portrait shows
Her gaze turned inward and her hands
In a delicate diffident pose,
Tiger-lilies lightly clasped.
Who shall say he understands
What fingers on flowers signed and masked?

Ten years are used and cast aside.
This year is evil more than most.
Those lights were false. For she remains,
Rising from all that she denied,
Like great parks on this hurried coast,
And statues through the dirty rains.

Rude now with pride and with humility
I come upon a true, false argument
That every love must die because the sea
And waves of love fail like an accident.
All things must flash away; with them, love, too.
All flesh is trash and not like truth or rock
—Shall pass away! even the famous blue
Is clouded over quickly as tick-tock!

But longer, lasting longer, is the good
I found by fumbling fearful, mostly lost,
Seeking forgiveness, much misunderstood,
And all the knowledge which the sun distorts.
—But if my hope is false, these gifts will be
Like pictures to the blind a mockery,
Or Mozart to the deaf an irony,
Useless, senseless, gratuitous vanity.

Who thrashed Goliath and whipped Caliban?
Let him appear and let his strength be known
In a new prodigy who snaps a stone,
Showing the dark horse underdog again
Winning against all odds and thrilling us
When bully braggart might is overthrown:
Samson and Cinderella set the tone,
They showed how virtue is victorious,

Their feats, as famous as the swaying waltz,
Make tyranny appear precarious.
—It is untrue. Such paradigms are false
In the early morning's waking consciousness:
We must be critics of success to see
What nothingness persists in victory.

## CHAPLIN UPON THE CLIFF, DINING ALONE

Again I put away a gold rush hope:
It was my eye deluded me, my hopeful eye
Which looked at sunlight flashing like a whip.
Still in the untouched blue the sparkling sky
In the early morning light makes promises
—Too much, too little!—outstretched endlessly.
Perhaps true angels' unheard choruses?
Or maybe but a simple senseless sea?

With this uncertainty, rocked by two waves,
I paddle with my hands a middle sea
In a small boat alone; and if my gaze
Is full of anxious curiosity,
One more illusion will not fool my eye
Before I hope again as foolishly!

## TWELFTH NIGHT, NEXT YEAR, A WEEK-END IN ETERNITY

We who hang our hearts up, like Christmas stockings,
Find in them broken tiles fallen from the roof,
For Claus surely exists, but the thumbprint markings,
On every gift and windfall, seem to be the proof
That his hands are dirty, his fingers inkstained, and his arms weak,
So that he often pauses, carrying his heavy bag.
—Yet often in the morning, although it too can flag,
When I welcome what will come next, above the clock's tick-tick
The soul is a bird which has suddenly stopped singing:
And listening and silent, and silent and listening, and listening and silent,
It attempts to understand what its waiting has meant.
Then I think dear Claus, whose sleigh-bells are ringing,
A sad clown in polka gown whom my applause
Will once more invigorate, before the coming wars.

## THE MORNING LIGHT FOR ONE WITH TOO MUCH LUCK

Sick and used Cambridge in the suck-
Ing sound of slow rain at dead dawn
Amid the sizzle sound of car and truck
As if continually thin cloth were torn,

Blue light, plum light, fading violet light,
And then the oyster light of the wool sky:
Is this not, after all, appropriate
Light for a long used poet such as I?

The steady juices of the rain fulfill
November, ember, ashen ageing youth:
Here, my dear poet, with weather, wit, and will,
And a long look you learned to like the truth!

## FIRST MORNING IS UNTRUE

First morning is untrue,
Then every hope is dead,
Faint light in the dark air,
When most I think of the blue,
Thinking the little I dare,
Abandoned to all care,
Capsized the heavy head,
Driven beyond old dread,
The morning faint or untrue,
A new world untrue, untrue!
Art, knowledge, and love betrayed
And the last hope lost in the blue.

O memory understood, in looking back!
This was my life amid the shocking guns
Of war far off and near. As one who runs
I was, as one, foot forward on the track,
Head turned, grotesque, loses like Orpheus
The girl gay, fey and frozen in the past,
Yet wins the smiles of beasts and knows, at last,
Touring the underworld brings happiness!

Moonlight upon the hatrack, picture, and clock,
Here have I come, here rule the modern powers.
—Forward with straining neck, darkness and lock
I open, doubled, transfixed looking back,
Glimpsing how valueless the flowing hours
Before this consciousness. Which stares and towers.

He calls, enchained, forced in the darkened lights,
Giraffes of light like hanged men on the street,
Instructed by one hundred thousand nights
Entering and suffering sepia deceit.
October, December, remember summer, save
Him from the left wrong side of his face.
Guilt, like eczema, he must fear and crave,
Untutored by the mind's sufficient grace.

"Here is my heart," he chants, "here is my head,
"And here its secret parts," as he gave to all
Fruits, flowers, candy boxed, and easy to lift,
And not the rotten apple, brown with dread,
Ruined by remorse and gnawed on since the Fall,
—Surprise because they shun the fearful gift!

The early morning always is untrue,
The self is nervous in a false distrust.
The mind knows once again how vague the blue,
And wades all memory because it must.
Leafshadows on the wall, carflights' flashed sleeves,
The city, sad and used, lies like a corpse
In the long silence as the first of leaves
Greenly, in August, to the brickwalk drops.

Now, midst the truths of silence, who believes
In noon, the city life, the thronging Square?
The present moment always is untrue!
Emotion and fantasy renew
The dreams the sleeper tries to criticize,
As light brings back old hope's ingenious lies.

This life is but fireworks at the fancy shore
Among the summer people, drinking gin,
Chilled by the vanity and senseless roar
Of breakers broken quicker than a pin,
By the moon broken, soaring and unheard,
—Thus we are tossed! by powers from afar,
By puns on rocks in Christ's most obscure word,
Or, when the moonlight glitters, by a star!

Look well and you will see there is no stay:
No one takes back a word, but once for all
What has been said can never be unsaid
No matter what trash and newness every day
The fresh years bring and break and take away:
This is the poet's power, this is his dread.

I sat amid flickering shadows of the war,
Sad about being sad (in this capital
Where thought and art arose once, beautiful).
In the soft bland hypnotic dark I saw
Two motion pictures show how boy meets girl,
How poor young man may win the boss' daughter
Although he constantly gets in hot water;
Then came the newsreel's circumstantial whirl.

Churchill nudged Roosevelt. With handsome glee
Roosevelt winked! Upon life's peak they played
(Power is pleasure, though anxious. Power is free!)
Mah-jong or pat-a-cake with history:
They swayed like elephants in the gaiety
And the enormity of their success!

O evening like a frieze, late light serene,
The city fades beneath your passing poise,
The heavy huddled buildings look like toys,
The silence murmurs in the trees' thick green.
The Square—Georgian façade, or that late French
Baroque dear to the victors in the Civil War—
Thins to a postcard's picayune décor,
As the racked traffic lurches in a trench.

This transience shall instruct us like a gift.
Secret and strong beneath the city lights
(Scattered like rice in evening's growth and drift),
Our being's sources like a myth arise
From depths like mothers or the starlight's heights,
Whence we shall sing beyond the city's lies.

## HOPE LIKE THE PHOENIX BREAST RISES AGAIN

Who sang and sang beyond the war insane
And still must sing? by his own self betrayed
As by the city's grand and gross façade,
The skyline's emptiness and broken chain,
The empty heights, America's success,
Vain numbers infinite and meaningless,
Which bring the rich and poor boredom or pain,

Who love to go to parties, joke,
Drink and tell stories, kiss on New Year's Eve,
Having the habits of a country folk
Beneath the city's dress. Who can believe
All will arise and sing with us? Of love, love
Unknown and fabulous in old New York.

74124

He named each child Orestes, hunted down.
Two years are lived and now he sees more truth,
The furies turned to mercies and the brown
Baked ghosts kind friends, weeping with ruth
Because he turned and looked at them and fled
No more their staring faces,fearing the past
Risen renewed in him as if the dead
Sins of the parent throve in the son's breast.

This is the way, to halt, turn, and go back
To look long at the crime, to know it well,
To walk with care upon the rotten track
As agonized as all the fools in hell
—Then, then, dénouement done, like a May sun
Forgiveness frees and blesses everyone.

Nothing that he expected but surprises,
Seeking surprise like one at Luna Park
(All the grand ohs as genuine as a claque,
Cigars and dolls, exploded booby prizes);
Given each thing except the thing he wanted
(Like a rich girl who wants to be a boy)
Though what he wanted was the joy of joy
—If it was that—since each desire counted

For naught but the false hope that here, at last! . . .
—And now? While new illusion shines and rains
Like a bad Spring, what famous game remains?
To praise unmasking and unmaskers, do
With love what they did, trying to be true,
Before the shows and sketches have been passed.

# THE SELF UNSATISFIED RUNS EVERYWHERE

Sunday and sunlight ashen on the Square,
Hard wind, high blue, and clouded pennant sky,
Fifth Avenue empty in the autumn air,
As if a clear photograph of a dead day.
It was the Lord's day once, solemn and full
—Now I in an aftermath, desire spent,
Move with a will appeased and see a gull,
Then gulls drop from an arch—scythes of descent!—

Having, I think, no wish beyond the foam
Toppling to them at each fresh exercise,
Knowing success like fountains, perhaps more wise
Than one who hesitantly writes a poem
—But who, being human, wishes to be a gull,
Knows nothing much, though birds are beautiful.

# LOOK, IN THE LABYRINTH OF MEMORY

Regard, O reader, how it is with me:
This year am I five thousand years of age,
Secure in Pharaoh's great society,
Like uncle Joseph, or a lesser mage.
This year will be the thirtieth eternity
The thirtieth time around the solar fire,
But if I count night watches, obviously
How I am aged in hope and dead desire!

For I am fifty years by sleepless toll:
And more than that! for every fresh event
Flashes upon the waiting wakeful soul
New light on what the past time might have meant:
And as we think of years, thinking like this,
Look, reader, how we stare at an abyss!

Today is a holiday in the Western heart,
—Three cheers, my dears, we celebrate the peace!
If not a true peace, since we now take part
In a new death, this too, my peers, shall cease,
And once more some will study works of art,
And some will seek for Sunday in the Park
And some will search new dangers in the heart,
And some will find that knowledge is an ark.

But what? False ease I speak, false as the blue:
This life will be the same, precarious,
Kind, stupid, sullen, rich and marvelous
(New works are possible because of this)
—All false as feeling, for poor consciousness
Loses each day what never will return to us.

## "I AM VERY EXQUISITELY PLEASED"

Shhhhhhhhhhhh!
Suddenly certainly the music box begins
Tinkling as for the birthday of a child,
The dogs and fates awhile are reconciled
By motions soft aloft as Zeppelins.
And stops, continues, stops or mounts because
Of powers strange as stars. Or good or bad
Or both, but mostly much misunderstood,
True, false, and fabulous like Santa Claus.

With incoherent braggadocio,
The storm flows overhead, beyond control,
—Yet who would play it like a radio
If but he could? These concerts to the soul
Have helpless strength like summer. One must go
Blindfolded and bewildered, groping and dumb,
Suspicious of the kingdom which has come.

"Why when you write do you most frequently
Look in your heart and stare at it both first
And last, half agonized by what you see
And half bemused, seeking what is accursed
Or blesséd in the past? And what demand
Is gratified?" I answered, hesitant
And slow: "I think I wish to understand
The causes of each great and small event

Chosen, or like thrown dice, an accident,
—My clumsiness each time I try to dance,
My mother's anger when I wore long pants:
For, as the light renews each incident,
My friends are free of guilt or I am free
Of self-accused responsibility."

SIXTEEN HUNDRED COPIES
OF THIS BOOK, DESIGNED BY
S. A. JACOBS, WERE PRINTED AT
THE GOLDEN EAGLE PRESS
MOUNT VERNON, NEW YORK
MCML